A Scholars Guide
To Zero Tuition and Maximum
Success

How I Received My Bachelor's and
Master's Degree For Free

D'Shyla M. Duncan

Copyright © [2025] D'Shyla M. Duncan

All rights reserved. No part of this book may be reproduced, stored in a retrieval system, or transmitted in any form or by any means electronic, mechanical, photocopying, recording, or otherwise without prior written permission from the author, except for brief quotations in reviews or as permitted by copyright law.

Published by D'Shyla M. Duncan

For inquiries, visit: www.shylathescholar.com

First Edition

ISBN 979-8-9926330-0-9 (Paperback)

ISBN 979-8-9926330-1-6 (Hardback)

Cover Design by Natalia A. Avery

This book is a work of nonfiction. While every effort has been made to ensure accuracy, the author and publisher assume no responsibility for errors or omissions. The content reflects the author's experiences and research and is not intended as professional, financial, or legal advice.

Printed in the United States of America

TABLE OF CONTENTS

PREFACE v

Chapter 1 1
PREPARATION 1
   QUICK TIPS FOR PREPARATION 12

Chapter 2 13
HOW TO FIND SCHOLARSHIPS 13
   QUICK TIPS FOR HOW TO FIND SCHOLARSHIPS 21

Chapter 3 22
FINANCIAL AID 22
   QUICK TIPS FOR FINANCIAL AID 29

Chapter 4 30
APPLICATION PROCESS 30

Chapter 5 42
NOW YOU WRITE 42
   QUICK TIPS FOR NOW YOU WRITE 50

Chapter 6 51
YOU HAVE TO WANT IT 51
   Acknowledgments 55
   RESOURCES & TIPS 56
      SITES TO FIND SCHOLARSHIPS 59

Appendix A 62

Appendix B 67

PREFACE

The inspiration for this book comes from my mother's unwavering support and motivation, which encouraged me to document my journey of graduating debt-free. I wanted to share my experience with others, particularly those who face financial barriers, including students from Black and Brown communities.

However, imposter syndrome began to creep in. I thought, "Why would anyone want to hear my tips?" "Who am I to give advice?" "I didn't even receive that much money." Constantly diminishing my light, I convinced myself it was useless, and no one would care or invest in the book.

It took the words of my husband to encourage me. He reminded me that I cannot defeat myself before I even start, nor should I fear the results. He assured me that this book is not useless and that those for whom it is intended will find value in it.

So, with that, I thank you for purchasing this book! Having successfully achieved a debt-free education, I feel a strong desire to pay it forward and provide practical advice to empower others to do the same.

I'd like to give you some insight about myself before we dive into the book. Before graduating high school, I was determined not to take out loans for college. I made up my mind and decided it wasn't an option. I learned about grants, scholarships, and fellowships and how to take advantage of every resource available to me. I discovered how to leverage FAFSA to maximize my grants.

Eventually, I received so much funding for my undergraduate studies that I got a refund because I had more money than I needed. During my undergraduate studies, I studied abroad in South Africa on the prestigious Benjamin A. Gilman Scholarship.

For my graduate studies, I was awarded a graduate assistantship that covered my Master's in Public Health. While working part-time in the university's Office of Fellowships, I learned even more about scholarships and fellowships. I gained valuable insight into what scholarship committees are looking for from the perspective of a reviewer and how they score applications.

I am proud to say that in this role, I was able to assist multiple students in securing scholarships and fellowships for studying, researching, and teaching abroad.

This book aims to serve as a comprehensive guide for students embarking on their educational journeys. Drawing from my own experiences, I offer valuable tips, tools, and resources that have been instrumental in my success. I hope this book will alleviate some of the challenges associated with finding scholarships and preparing for college, providing you with a sense of ease during this important phase of your life. I must note that while this book is based on my experiences, it is by no means intended to be the only route or set of options for graduating debt-free. Everyone's circumstances are unique, and various strategies and avenues exist for obtaining financial assistance. However, I sincerely hope that the insights and strategies I share in this book will prove helpful to you on your journey.

Throughout this book, I will provide all the tools, resources, and strategies I utilized to secure over $100,000 worth of scholarships and grants for my undergraduate and graduate studies. So, take notes, highlight important sections, and keep this book close during your scholarship search. Refer to it whenever you need guidance. I hope you learn something new and, most importantly, that you receive scholarships for your post-secondary studies.

While this book may seem geared toward middle and high school students, the tips provided are also applicable to graduate students, those currently in college, and anyone looking to study abroad.
Sending blessings your way for your scholarship hunt!

Chapter 1

PREPARATION

Growing up, I was taught that if you excel in school, scholarships will come to you when you're ready to graduate. While this may be true for some, it was not my experience. Throughout my K-12 education, I was a stellar student, earning all A's. Despite maintaining a high Grade Point Average *(GPA is a number used to represent a student's academic performance)*[4] and being involved in extracurricular activities, I quickly realized that scholarships would not simply fall into my lap by my junior year of high school. It became clear that if I wanted to secure scholarships, I needed to be proactive and intentional in my approach.

Looking back, I realize that I laid the groundwork for scholarship success early on by attending an early college and participating in extracurricular activities. Many people think scholarships are only about grades, but that's not the whole story. Scholarship committees also consider a student's character, involvement, leadership skills, and more.

So, what makes you stand out? What's your GPA? Are you an athlete? A mentor? Part of a club? Do you volunteer or have a job? These are all important things to think about throughout your education, especially before you start high school. That's because scholarship committees will look at your involvement and performance when you apply.

Aim to keep your GPA at 3.5 or higher, since many major scholarships require at least a 3.0. But as I mentioned earlier, good grades aren't the only thing that matters when it comes to getting scholarships.

Get involved! Whether you volunteer in your community, serve as a leader at church, or hold the position of class president. Scholarship committees want to see that you are not only an exceptional student but also a rising leader. Find activities that you enjoy, and that will benefit you while looking good on your resume.

For example, I volunteered throughout my high school experience at local shelters, hospitals, daycares, and my high school. I made sure to be professional and build strong relationships with my supervisors. These connections were sought out because of my genuine passion for community service, and they also served as valuable resume builders. When I needed a recommendation letter, I felt confident asking, knowing I had performed my duties efficiently. I was punctual and friendly and made it a point for my supervisors to get to know me.

It is important to note that you should not engage in community service or other activities solely because you think you will gain something in return. While thinking about your future is essential, it's equally important to build genuine relationships, pursue what you enjoy, and remain consistent. Scholarship committees can be turned off if they see that you participated in activities without commitment.

How can they trust you to fulfill their requirements and maintain their scholarship if you aren't dedicated? How will they know that you were involved in those activities because you genuinely enjoyed them rather than just checking boxes for personal gain?

It's just as important to build strong relationships with your high school teachers and staff. They can be your first mentors and play a significant role in your scholarship search, providing recommendation letters and helping you find suitable scholarships. You want them to know you as a student and a person. However, don't force these relationships to get letters. Let them develop naturally; genuine connections with your teachers and staff are crucial. You can continue communicating with them even after graduation, and they can become lifelong mentors.

While doing well in school and participating in activities is important, it's equally important to research, plan, and prepare thoroughly. By being proactive, you can increase your chances of getting scholarships that will support your education. Now, let's explore other ways to prepare for your scholarship search. A successful search requires a proactive and well-planned approach. Start preparing early, even before your senior year. I began researching scholarships the summer before my senior year, using methods like bookmarking websites, organizing computer folders, and collecting scholarship flyers. This helped me gather valuable information about scholarships before applications opened.

By conducting thorough scholarship research ahead of time, you gain the advantage of reviewing the specific requirements for each scholarship. These requirements may include eligibility criteria, minimum GPA, essay length, due dates, potential recommendation letters, and the responsibilities associated with maintaining the scholarship. Please note that some of the scholarships you research may not have this information publicized so far in advance, but you can still determine if it is a good fit for you by reading the description of the scholarship opportunity. Nevertheless, preparing in advance allows you to explore a wide range of scholarships and determine which ones align best with your goals and aspirations.

Review the essay prompts (if required) for the scholarships and write them down or copy them into a Word document so that you can start to brainstorm potential answers. Look up the past winners of the scholarships. Read their biography and, if provided, look over their essay answers so that you can get an idea of what a winning essay sounds like, looks like, and includes. You want to gain as much information as you can about the scholarships; this way, you know what is expected of you. During this preparation process, I found that peak scholarship time is between August through December. During this time, the bulk of scholarships will be made available, and they will likely be due from October to January. Many students can miss out because some think most scholarships open closer to their enrollment in college. However, this is not the case for a lot of major scholarships. You may find yourself applying for scholarships before committing to a college. That is fine; you do not have to be committed to start researching and applying for scholarships.

Another important aspect to consider during the preparation process is the Scholastic Assessment Test (SAT) or the American College Test (ACT). While the tests differ, both are standardized tests used for college admission in the United States. Though I believe a single test shouldn't solely determine scholarship eligibility or college admissions, it sometimes does. I was a straight-A student in high school; I had a 3.95 GPA. However, I received a 990 on my SAT, and I thought for sure that I was a failure. I thought that all people would care about was how I did on the SAT instead of considering how well of a student I was. Unfortunately, this was true, as several scholarships disqualified me despite my academic success because of my SAT score. I was so devastated because I did not think that I was going to be able to receive scholarships. My state changed its exam from the ACT to the SAT during my testing year, which left my entire cohort feeling unprepared. We had spent our entire K-12 education preparing for the ACT, only to be told at the last minute that we had to take the SAT instead. A whirlwind, I know! Remember that you can always choose to retake the SAT or ACT if you want to.

I think a very important factor that helped me to receive scholarships was being in a dual enrollment program (*Dual Enrollment programs require the student to attend college, either online or on-campus, earning credit for both college and high school graduation requirements*)[1]. My high school was part of an early college program, which allowed me to graduate with three Associate degrees before finishing high school. Now, I realize that not everyone goes to an early college or may not know how to access this opportunity. I urge you to consider researching dual-enrollment opportunities in your area. While it is never too late, I recommend deciding to attend an early college program before starting high school. This way, you can reap the full benefits of the program by being involved in it for your entire high school career.

Many people also decide to take Advanced Placement (AP) courses (*The AP Program offers college-level courses and exams that you can take in high school*)[6]; if they do not go to a high school with a dual-enrollment program because it can be cheaper than dual enrolment and people assume this opportunity will reap the same benefits. However, I highly suggest dual enrollment over AP courses because AP courses can be just as demanding and time-consuming as actual college classes but are not college courses. Additionally, with AP courses, to receive college credit, you must pass the test associated with that class. So, your ability to receive college credit is not based on how you did in that class over the semester but on how well you did on one test.

Having advanced courses on your transcript and doing well in them can be an alternative factor in determining your college eligibility, aside from your SAT/ACT scores, if you didn't score as well as you had hoped. This shows scholarship committees and college admissions offices that you're prepared for college, since you've already taken and excelled in advanced courses. Not all scholarships require SAT/ACT scores, and many colleges now let students choose whether to include them without penalty. So, if you're worried about your scores, you have a better chance of getting in. You're no longer held back by one test that determines your future.

Okay, take a breath! I hope that wasn't too much because this is only the beginning. Hang with me a little longer so we can continue to talk about my path to scholarships.

QUICK TIPS FOR PREPARATION

❖ Start Early.

❖ Your SAT/ACT score does not define you. You can still get scholarships!

❖ A lot of great scholarships set their due dates from October to January.

❖ Set reminders in your phone for when the scholarship application opens so you will be alerted!

❖ Inquire with your high school about taking AP courses or dual enrollment (dual enrollment over AP if possible).

❖ Go to an accredited university or college for your undergraduate studies.

.

Chapter 2

HOW TO FIND SCHOLARSHIPS

GENERAL SCHOLARSHIP SEARCH

When searching for scholarships, it's important to utilize all available resources to find as many opportunities as possible. Sign up for different scholarship websites such as Fast web, Course Hero, Scholarships.com, and Scholarships America. These platforms are user-friendly and allow you to answer questions or create a profile to match you with scholarships for which you qualify.

Google is usually our go-to place for everything, including scholarships. But, finding scholarships through Google search can be tricky at times. I've learned that searching in different ways can get you different results and uncover scholarship opportunities that didn't show up before. For instance, if you're looking for scholarships for a graduating high school senior who's a girl, you could try searching for "Scholarships for women graduating high school," "college scholarships for women," or "Scholarships for high school seniors." It may seem tedious, but rephrasing your search can really help you find different scholarships. Another way to use Google is to visit your state government's financial aid webpage. For example, searching "Scholarships in Michigan" will take you to your state government's financial aid page, which lists all the available scholarships and grants.

Additionally, I recommend asking people around you for help in finding scholarship opportunities. This includes your parents, friends, school staff, and administrators. Many scholarships go unnoticed because people aren't actively looking for them or don't know they exist. Use all the resources available to you so you can apply for every opportunity that comes your way.

For example, the company my dad worked for offered a scholarship, and I was eligible to apply because he was an employee. Additionally, my parents' insurance company offered a scholarship for members, which I qualified for. The list goes on; my credit union, my church, and my high school offered scholarships. So, be sure to ask your parents if their jobs, insurance companies, banks, etc. offer scholarship opportunities.

Moreover, I went to my school counselor's office frequently to ask her if she knew about any potential scholarship opportunities. She would send me emails about scholarship opportunities or give me a flyer when I stopped by her office. I utilized all available resources to maximize my scholarship opportunities.

Ask about local or statewide scholarships because you will be surprised by the scholarship opportunities right in your city or state. I feel that we are often only encouraged to apply for the full-ride scholarships or prestigious national scholarships that everyone knows about. While I do think that you should apply for these scholarships. I encourage you not to overlook smaller scholarships or non-renewable scholarships (<u>*non-renewable, meaning the scholarship money is a one-time payment, not yearly*</u>)[2]. All scholarship money is worth researching and applying for, whether it is for $5,000 or $500. Please do not overlook scholarship opportunities because the amount of money may seem small; I promise everything adds up!

Note that sometimes renewable scholarships *(renewable, meaning the scholarship money will continue to be provided for 4 years of undergraduate study or until you graduate, whichever comes first)*[2] may require you to maintain a certain GPA or take a certain number of credits to keep your scholarship. For example, I received a scholarship that required recipients to complete a yearly renewal form that required GPA, college status, and uploading official college transcripts. This way, they could assess how I did that academic year and whether I qualified to get the scholarship renewed. So, make sure you are keeping your grades up and doing your best to keep your scholarship money.

INSTITUTIONAL SCHOLARSHIPS

The search for scholarships specific to a college can be a different process. I advise you to write down a list of your top five schools and research the scholarship opportunities they offer that you qualify for. If you know what you want to major in, see what scholarships they are providing and the criteria necessary to receive them. What is your hometown?

Sometimes, college scholarships will be specific to certain communities. What is your ethnicity? Sometimes, colleges will have scholarships specifically for people of certain ethnic groups. Do keep in mind that many institutional scholarships may require you to attend certain events, write papers, check in with an advisor, and more throughout your time at the university.

For example, I went to Central Michigan University for my undergraduate studies and received their Multicultural Advancement Scholarship (MAC)[5]. The MAC scholarship is a cultural diversity scholarship. MAC scholars were required to attend 2 events for each cultural month. Such as Black History Month, Hispanic Heritage Month, Asian American and Pacific Islander Heritage Month, and so on. We were required to attend study tables every week to complete our homework and take cultural diversity classes.

Additionally, we had to maintain a minimum GPA of 2.5 and enroll in at least 12 credit hours. This is an example of what the requirements for certain college scholarships could look like.

Merit-based college scholarships *(A merit-based scholarship considers applicants' academic records, leadership experience, and background. Unlike a need-based scholarship, merit-based scholarships do not consider financial need)*[2] are also an opportunity to receive funding for college. Usually, you do not have to apply for merit-based scholarships. Merit-based scholarships may have requirements like a 3.5 GPA or higher, 1300 or higher on the SAT, 24 or higher on the ACT, athletic achievements, volunteerism, etc. You will be considered for these scholarships when you apply to the university and if you meet the criteria.

Also consider your bandwidth and what you can manage, as it's important to meet all the requirements for your scholarships while also excelling in school. It's not impossible! I recommend getting a planner, setting reminders, using your calendar, or adopting whatever method works best for you to stay organized and keep track of scholarship deadlines and requirements. The last thing you want is to work hard to secure your scholarships, only to miss renewal deadlines or fall behind on requirements. Time management, planning, and organization are key.

QUICK TIPS FOR HOW TO FIND SCHOLARSHIPS

- ❖ Rephrasing your scholarship search in Google is important.

- ❖ Some scholarships require certain services to maintain the award.

- ❖ Keep track of your scholarship renewal requirements every year.

- ❖ Utilize your resources in high school: counselors, teachers, and principals.

- ❖ Write down your top five schools and research their scholarship opportunities.

Chapter 3
FINANCIAL AID

Your parents' income plays an important role in your financial aid experience. Their earnings can significantly impact the amount of scholarship or grant money you receive. If your parents are not married, consider using the income of the parent who earns less when applying for the Free Application for Federal Student Aid (FAFSA)[3]. Students whose parents are divorced or were never married have the option to include only one parent's income. Nonetheless, always check FAFSA's rules and regulations for yourself via their website. Since policies may change, I want to ensure you comply to avoid risking your funding.

Without proper planning and strategies, college can lead to substantial debt. By making this simple adjustment mentioned above with my parent's income. We were able to reduce their costs from nearly $2,000 for my first year to having my second year in college fully covered.

Remember to apply for FAFSA as soon as it opens, and reapply every year you're in college. This ensures you'll continue to receive scholarship funding, grant money, and loans. There are three ways your scholarship money can be distributed: direct deposit or a check made out to you, a check sent to you made out to the school, or directly to the school. Regardless, promptly give your scholarship money to financial aid. You can do this by visiting the financial aid office with your checks or, if the money is directly deposited, sending it from your bank account to the financial aid office through your school's website. If the scholarship committee sends the money directly to your school, it will go straight to financial aid, and you won't need to do anything – the money will simply appear on the financial aid portal via your school's website.

Although scholarship funds can be deposited or sent directly to you, it's important to remember that this is not free money. Ensure that you are accountable and responsible for your scholarship money by sending it to your financial aid office promptly. The scholarship committee has entrusted you with these funds to support your education, so make sure you utilize the money for its intended purpose.

BUDGETING

Creating a budget is very important to keep track of how much scholarship money you have received and how much money you still need to pay for college. When you have your top five colleges/universities in mind or have committed to your college/university, take note of the total cost of tuition plus room and board for one semester (*room and board meaning your college dorm and meal plan costs*). That total amount multiplied by two is the overall amount that you need for the entire first academic year of college. For example, if the college tuition is $9,000 and the room and board is $4,945 for the first semester. This means that the first semester is $13,945. College is split into two semesters for a full academic year. Therefore, if the previous expenses applied to you, this would mean that you'd need a total of $27,890 for your first academic year of school to be paid in full (this total does not include the cost of books or other resources that may be needed, as that can vary).

I recommend creating a Microsoft Excel sheet, Google Sheets, or a table in Microsoft Word, or even going old-school by writing everything out. It's essential to keep track of all the expenses related to your college education. This way, as your scholarships start rolling in, you can monitor the funds you have for school and your remaining balance. I promise this will save you a lot of headaches and help you stay organized.

My mom created my budget in Microsoft Word and kept track of everything related to my college funds. If you have a family member who is great with finances, I recommend asking them for help in creating a budget and tracking your expenses, however, if you don't have anyone to assist you, no worries! You'll find a copy of my budget for my first academic year in college in the next few pages. You can use it as a guide to create your own. I've added comments to certain items to provide context.

[Comment box: Leadership Safari was an orientation experience for first-year students (amount not included in tuition or room/board costs, my mom was just keeping track of all expenses).]

[Comment box: Keep track of due dates. Sometimes scholarship money may come after certain due dates. This is okay as colleges/universities usually allow you to defer payment by simply filling out a form.]

D'Shyla Awarded Scholarships Budget

Tuition is due by September 8, 2017 or late fees will occur

Tuition Only (12) credit hours	Room and Board	Total Cost each Semester
Fall: $ 5025.00	Standard: 14 meal 250 flex Plan: $4,670.00	$ 9,695
Spring: $ 5025.00	Standard: 14 meal 250 flex Plan: $4,670.00	$ 9,695 (year total: $19,390)
Leadership Safari Cost:	$ 50.00	

Renewable Scholarships Received

Name	Awarded Amount	Renew	G.P.A Requirements to keep Scholarship	Payments sent out	Fall	Spring
CMU Multicultural	4125	Up to 4 years	Must maintain an overall 3.0	CMU Put on Account	2062.5	2062.5
Foresters	2000	Up to 3 years	Must maintain an overall 3.0	Payment in July/ August	1000	1000
Wilsterman	5000	Up to 4 years	Must maintain an overall 3.0 Student must arrange with school to send grade after each semester	Payment of the award will be made directly to school	2500	2500
PEPSICO Renewal form sent in December	2000	Up to 3 years	Must maintain an overall 3.0	Lump Sum Payment August 1st Mailed to student with school name on it.	1000	1000
Total	$13,125				$ 6562.5	$6562.5

[Comment box: All of your scholarship money will be split in half for each semester. As you can see here this scholarship was for $4,125. It was divided between fall and winter semester to $2062.5]

One-Time Scholarships Awarded

Name	Total Awarded Amount	Fall	Spring
Youth Awardee/Sojourner Truth	$500.00 (send 250 for fall/ 250 for Spring)	250	250
New Creation Scholarship	$ 500 (250/250)	250	250
CMU Grant	$ 875 (437.5/437.5)	437.5	437.5
GISD Retired Teacher Stipend	$ 500.00 (250/250)	250	250
MMC Principal Award	$ 400.00 (200/200)	200	200
AmeriCorps	$ 1230.68 (615.34/615.34)	615.34	615.34
Genesee Opportunity Stipend	$ 650 (325/325) FA Representative: Penny stated will have payment split between both semesters (8/21/2017)	325	325
Total:	$ 4,655.68	2327.84	2327.84

There was an option to have some of the cost waived for this orientation experience. If you have any opportunities to get costs waived for orientations or other required experiences, take advantage to save more money!

Leadership Safari 60/40 Scholarship Cost: $ 125.00
College Pays: $ 75

Total Funding Received from Grants and Scholarships
$ 17,780.68

Fall: $ 8890.34	Spring: $ 8890.34
Fall Need: $ 854.66	Spring Need: $ 854.66

Loans if Needed

	Unsubsidized Loans	Amount Needed	Amount Needed
		Fall: 804.66	Spring:
	Suggested Amount based on need $ 5,500	Total Needed to Borrowed: 1609.32	

Work-Study Employment Funding

Fall		1300	Employment on Campus
Summer		1300	Employment on Campus

Although, I did not take out any loans for my college education. My mom kept track of all expenses and possibilities. These were the loan amounts offered to me on the financial aid portal. The amount goes down as you receive more scholarship money. These loans have to be accepted by you to cover your college expenses. You DO NOT have to accept these loans if you do not need to.

On the FASFA application click yes for work-study. You want to have the option to work during your college experience if you want or need to.

QUICK TIPS FOR FINANCIAL AID

- ❖ Fill out FAFSA on time.

- ❖ Create a budget to keep track of your scholarships and your overall college expenses.

- ❖ Use the parent with the least amount of income for the FAFSA form to try and receive the most amount of grant funding possible.

- ❖ Three ways scholarship money is allocated: Direct Deposit, Check (made out to you or school), or sent directly to your school.

Chapter 4

APPLICATION PROCESS

The application process is one of the most important aspects of many scholarships, alongside the essay portion, as this is where you provide all the necessary information to submit your application. When applying for scholarships, the process can vary in length depending on the award amount and the prestige of the scholarship. Time management and dedication are crucial for ensuring this process goes smoothly, especially when completing lengthy applications.

Scholarship applications are not particularly difficult; the hard part is completing them. You will find scholarship applications that are very quick and easy, in which you can finish them in one sitting. However, some applications can take over a week, maybe even over a month, to complete because of the things required. Longer applications may require letter(s) of recommendation, official high school transcripts, resume, essay(s), and more. Therefore, you must plan accordingly and manage your time when completing your applications. I do not recommend trying to complete a long application in one day. In my experience, this can cause overstimulation, stress, and burnout. So, take your time and start early; if you do this, there will be no need to rush through the process.

I recommend creating a schedule for when you will apply for scholarships. Write down your scholarship applications and when they are due, then arrange them according to how long you think they will take and the due dates. Prioritize longer scholarship applications and those with earlier deadlines. For example, if you have an application that requires two letters of recommendation and three essays. I recommend reaching out to the people you want to do your recommendation letter immediately via email. Give them an overview of the scholarship and what it is about, then ask if they are willing to write the letter for you. Reaching out very early allows your potential recommenders ample time to complete the letter. Then you can begin to create your schedule around applying. You can work on a long application for about an hour, then a short one, and alternate like this as you complete scholarships or add new applications to complete. Do not complete them all in one day, and do not sit in front of your computer for hours. Take a break and relax. Hence why you start early so you can avoid late nights and cramming. Scholarships with longer application processes usually have an option to save and come back to it later.

    On the next few pages, there will be an actual copy of one of my longer scholarship applications. Hopefully, this can give you an idea of what some applications may ask for.

Applicant Information

***First Name**
D'Shyla

***Last Name**
Hodge

***Address 1**
█████████████

Address 2

***City**
█████████

***State**
█

***Zip**
████

***Telephone where you may best be reached**
████████

***Email Address**
███████████████

School

***What high school are you graduating from?**
Mott Middle College High School

If Other, list here:

***Month/Year of Graduation or Anticipated Month/Year of Graduation**
June/2017

Enter the name, address and phone number of the school(s) you will attend, or are likely to attend, after high school:

***School Name**
Central Michigan University

***School Address Line 1**
1200 S. Franklin St

School Address Line 2

*School City
Mt Pleasant

*School State
MI

*School Zip
48859

School Name

School Address Line 1

School Address Line 2

School City

School State

School Zip

*What program of study or major are you interested in?
The program of study that I am going into is Biology/Pre-Medical Studies. Since I was 7 years old because I love people, science, and learning new things about how the human body operates.

*Do you have activities outside of the classroom? Do you work, volunteer, have responsibilities at home or elsewhere? If so, describe these activities and approximately how much time you devote to each activity described per week. These may include but are not limited to time devoted to extracurricular activities, community service, family, business, performing arts, creative arts, science, including computer science, economics, agriculture, animal husbandry, religion, politics, charity, literature, philosophy and medicine. Please list and discuss these, the affect they have had on you and others in your family and /or community and how they have affected your studies, positively and negatively.

Outside of school I have tried to always dedicate my time to community outreach, extra-curricular activities, groups etc. I have volunteered at Hurley Medical Center where I received a certificate for completing over 100 hours. I have also volunteered at many different establishments like Whaley's Children Center, The Humane Society, Shelter of Flint, Restore Habitat for Humanity, Mott Middle College, New Creation Church of God, The Crim Festival of Races, Civic Heights Church of God in Christ, Carriage Town Ministries etc. and I have accumulated over 200 hours of community service. I currently am a part of two groups at my church, New Creation Church of God, that both have a focus of unity, leadership, sisterhood, and growth in Christ. The groups are The Girls of Distinction and Girls of Gory dance ministry, which I have been a member of for 7 years. The Girls of Distinction promotes leadership, volunteerism, learning, and growth in your walk as a young woman in Christ. We meet every 2 weeks on Wednesday at church to discuss ways to reach out to the community and serve God through our giving. The Girls of Glory dance ministry, encourages young women to show their praise and honor for God through dance. We meet every Monday to practice and we have done many different styles of dance such as praise, hip hop, and ballet. I love reaching out into my community and showing my appreciation in any way that I can. Academically I am also an ambassador for the National Society of High School Scholars and a member of Phi Theta Kappa honor society at Mott Community College. Dedicating my time to each of these activities has helped me not only as a student to study harder, stay focus, and prioritize my time to balance learning with extra-curricular activities. But, it has shown me how to be grateful, humble, generous, caring, and compassionate towards others.

*Have you worked during high school?
No

If you answered yes to the question above, please complete the following. Where have you worked? Give approximate dates and who you worked for during the reported dates.

What were your duties?

Did your duties change and if so, how?

Approximately how many hours per week did you work, on average?

Please click here and have your immediate supervisor complete the "Applicant Work Evaluation".

Please upload your "Applicant Work Evaluation".

If you were self employed, describe your most valuable experiences. You may attach a statement from a customer if you wish. Include the customer's name and address and have the customer sign the statement.

Please upload your "Customer Statement" here.

*Plese list and discuss how your work has affected you and others in your family and how it has affected your studies, positively and negatively and your outlook on education and the work or career paths you may pursue.

I have never worked a paid job while being in school. However, I completed a 60-hour internship for my school while also being enrolled in school simultaneously. I completed my internship as a graduation requirement for my high school (Mott Middle College) at Hurley Medical Center. I worked in the outpatient clinic two days a week and I would say It impacted my studies in a positive way. It helped me learn how to prioritize my time, be more flexible and show endurance. My family was supportive throughout my entire internship and they also saw positive changes in certain areas of my life. Completing my internship prepared me for an actual job because it taught me how to stay alert, listen and focus on whatever task I had to complete. My internship also helped me decide what career in medicine I want to pursue which is a Family Physician. My internship helped in choosing my career choice because family physicians attended to many different types of people and are faced with different task every day. My internship prepared me for this by helping me learn how to be versatile and how to handle any situation as they come.

*List any awards or recognition you have received. List and briefly describe any creations you have presented, displayed, exhibited, peformed; articles, advertisements or other items you have had published or broadcast; speeches, lectures or presentations you have made or been involved in. If you haven't received any, please enter "None".

Here are the following awards and recognition I have received during my high school education:
- I have been on the Mott Community College dean's list consecutively for the past two years.
- I have been on the honor roll at Mott Middle College since my enrollment in September 2012
- I'm ranked 3rd in my high school graduating class.
- I have received a certificate from the Hurley Medical Center volunteer director for doing over 100 hours of volunteer work.
- I have been asked to speech at my high school graduation
- I have been nominated for the Paul Karr award at Mott Community College

Here is a list of presentations/ speeches I have done:
- In a Public Speaking course, I created Informative speeches and presentations about Breast cancer treatments and the importance of Safe Sex.
- In a Child Psychology course, I did a presentation on Mass Media and the effects it has on children.

*If you were absent from school more than 6 days in any academic year please explain why. If this doesn't apply please enter N/A.

N/A

*Have there been circumstances that you feel have prevented you from reaching your full academic or training potential, such as illness (you, family, etc.), work responsibilities, family responsibilities or other issues? Please describe.

Thankfully at this point in my academic career, I have been blessed not to have had any barriers such as illnesses within my system to hinder my education. I must note that my family support has always taught me to make my education top priority. I have learned also that I must have a plan and stick with to be successful in my accomplishments. The support I have received from my family has given me the opportunity to stay focus and strive harder not only academically but in every aspect of my life. All the support I have received over the years has helped me to mature and grow into the young women I am today. However, I do recognize that certain barriers and or circumstances may arise at any time that can prevent people for reaching their full potential. Therefore, I have always been mindful never to take my education for granted and always strive to do my best. My goal is to always encompass everything I have learned from my family and mentors in achieving my educational goals with diligence, focus, and patience.

*How, when combined with other resources, scholarships, grants, etc. will a grant from the Trust meaningfully assist you financially?

Receiving the Wilsterman Scholarship Trust would help tremendously in funding my college education because although I have received some scholarships and I'm currently awaiting the results of several others, receiving this scholarship would help pay for a great deal of my college expenses. Being awarded this scholarship is very important to me because I want to alleviate as much debt towards my college education as I can. My family does not have the financial resources to provide to help pay for my college education because I still have two younger brothers who live at home. Also, if I am awarded this scholarship combined with others it could help with getting my school supplies such as books, pencils, journals, room and board etc. Getting this scholarship would help support my college education and I definitely need all of the financial support I can get. I have applied for several scholarships but most of the scholarships are not renewable. That is why I am hoping to be a recipient of the Wilsterman trust scholarship because it assures that I will have constant money coming in for my college education.

If you wish, you may describe any other information about yourself that you may think helpful to the Advisory Committee but was not requested above.

I am hardworking, diligent, focused, and I take my education very seriously. I am very determined to further my education at a 4 year university and if chosen as a recipient of the Wilsterman Trust scholarship I can promise that I will sustain my GPA so that I can continue to receive this scholarship. I will also be very grateful and appreciative if chosen because I truly need all of the financial support that I can receive. Thank you so much for this opportunity and I hope to hear from you all soon!

Resources & Expenses

The table below is intended to tell us how you intend to pay for your education and must be completed.

Grants are sought to be made to those students for whom it would not be insignificant financial help and need must be demonstrated. Please provide information about your resources below: Please note that all other scholarships, grants or similar funds from others you are expecting to receive, have received or have applied for must be disclosed. As more information becomes available to you, you must update this information and we may contact you for verification before awarding assistance.

It is our hope that to the extent possible you can minimize or eliminate the need for loans and the debt that goes with them. Loans you have applied for, or intend to, will not generally be counted as resources that would disqualify you from receiving assistance from the Wilsterman Foundation.

RESOURCES

*Personal Savings of Applicant
$0.00

*Family Financial Contributions (Include only what your family has already designated as educational funds intended for you)
$0.00

*Scholarships Received
$5,500.00

*Scholarships Expected (do not include the Wilsterman Scholarship Trust)
$15,750.00

*Federal Aid / Grants
$0.00

*State Aid / Grants
$0.00

*Other Resources (Please describe below. Enter "0", if not applicable)
$0.00

Please describe Other Resources:

TOTAL RESOURCES
$21,250.00

EXPENSES

*Annual Tuition
$12,150.00

*Annual Books, Fees & Education Supplies
$1,000.00

*Annual Room & Board
$9,406.00

*Annual Estimated Transportation
$938.00

*Miscellaneous/Other (Please describe below. Enter "0", if not applicable)
$1,000.00

Please describe Entertainment/Miscellaneous Expenses:
I will need to purchase school supplies and personal things such as toiletries, pencils, pens, folders, journals, calculators, scrantons, blue books, etc. This list is not exhaustive depending on the courses and special supplies needed to fulfill the courses within the semesters.

TOTAL EXPENSES
$24,494.00

Narrative

If your resources shown above do not equal your expenses, how do you intend to make up the difference?
My goal is to apply for work-study and other employment opportunities on campus to help pay for my college expenses.

If there are additional circumstances not covered in the table above that may affect your finances for education, please indicate what circumstances you believe may be applicable. Include amounts, indicating also whether they are known or estimated.

QUICK TIPS FOR APPLICATION PROCESS

- ❖ Do not rush.

- ❖ Take a break.

- ❖ Start early; set reminders and alarms for scholarship openings and deadlines.

- ❖ Ask for letters of recommendation immediately, if needed.

Chapter 5
NOW YOU WRITE

I know writing essays isn't everyone's favorite task, but it's essential when applying for scholarships and grants. While not all scholarship applications require essays, many that you encounter during your search will. The essay portion is your opportunity to respond to the prompts provided by the scholarship committee and sell yourself. The key to writing winning scholarship essays is to answer the prompts in a way that captivates your reader.

You must be able to write in a way that compels your readers, engages them, and demonstrates why you are the perfect candidate for the award. My writing process begins by opening Microsoft Word on my laptop, pasting the essay prompts from the scholarship application into the document, and then starting to write. This approach helps me kick off my drafting process. I prefer to write down my initial thoughts and then edit, add, and refine them over time. If this method doesn't work for you, that's perfectly fine.

Do what feels best for you to achieve the best results. If you don't consider yourself a strong writer or struggle to come up with ideas, don't worry. Try writing out the scholarship prompts on a piece of paper or your laptop, and then write sentences or phrases that start to answer them. For example, if the prompts are "Tell us about yourself" and "What does leadership mean to you?", you could start by writing down where you're from, a passion you have, your desired major, and why. For the second prompt, you could write about someone you admire or a time you were in a leadership role. These answers will be the core message you want to convey to the scholarship committee. Next, think about how you can expand on these answers and tell a story about how you came to that conclusion. For instance, if you wrote that you want to major in dance because you've loved it since kindergarten, tell a story by explaining how you started dancing, who inspired you, what style of dance you like, what dance means to you, and your future career goals related to dance.

Another method I recommend for writing an essay, especially if the prompt isn't specific or isn't provided, is the 3 W's (Who, What, and Why). The 3 W's are a very simplified version of writing tips I provide to help people who may not consider themselves skilled writers. These tips are easy to follow and understand and can be applied to all types of essays not just to scholarship essays. The 3 W's are as follows: 1) Who are you? Provide background information about yourself that applies to the scholarship. 2) What have you done? Explain the activities or accomplishments that you believe qualify you for the scholarship. 3) Why do you want the scholarship? Or why should the organization invest in you? Explain why you believe you should receive the scholarship.

The goal is to bring the scholarship committee into your world. They don't know you, so you want to make the best first impression. This is your opportunity to paint a vivid picture based on the prompts provided, showing them who you are and why you deserve the scholarship.

Answer the essay prompts! I know it can be easy to go off into a flow of writing but make sure you are sticking to the topic provided and giving the scholarship committee exactly what they asked for. Especially if you have a limit of 1 to 2 pages, you must tell your story and be sure to answer the questions fully. You may be tempted to add other details, but if it is not relevant to the topic, essential to the story, or fails to answer the prompt, then omit it. Every part of your story may not be feasible for the limits they have, so write strategically. Use the writing tips I provided and answer the questions, but still bring forth a compelling story within the page limits. As for longer essay lengths, the same rules apply, but this is when you can dig deep into the story you want to tell and create a full-circle moment within your essay.

The essay portion is important; this is their introduction to who you are, how you think and feel, your vision, etc. Do not cheat yourself out of this opportunity by rushing the process. If you prioritize your time and start early, you will have plenty of time to write your essay. You will think of new things to add or delete throughout your essay-writing process, so allow yourself the appropriate amount of time for your ideas to flow.

All great writers have many drafts, edits, and proofreaders because they want to produce the best essay possible. When you feel you have written everything, answered the essay prompts, and produced your best work. Read over your essay, check for grammatical or punctuation errors, and even have your computer read the essay out loud to you so you can see how the essay flows. After that, send your essay to people who you trust to read it over and provide you with feedback about what can be improved. I recommend emailing it to your English teacher, History teacher, counselor, and many other people that you know are great writers. You can never have too many eyes on your essays; I recommend emailing them to at least 3 people so you can get many different opinions. When you receive the feedback, make the suggested corrections, and then send it back. When your reviewers tell you that they think your essay is in great condition, now you can upload it to your application and submit it. I recommend that you set a due date for yourself to have your essay done so that you can start to email it out for review. For example, if the scholarship deadline is May 30th, I would like to have my essay done by April 20th. This may seem early, but I like to get things done and have ample amounts of time to do my final edits. You would send it to your reviewers, and this gives them a lot of time to review it because you must remember that your teachers and counselors have other responsibilities. So, be courteous to them and email your essays at least 3 to 4 weeks before the deadline. Consequently, they will have ample time to review, and when you get feedback, you will have enough time to make corrections.

You might be thinking, "Wait, D'Shyla, do I really need to write 15 essays for 15 scholarship applications?" Not necessarily. As I mentioned earlier, not all scholarship applications require essays. Plus, I'm a big fan of reusing essays. If you're applying to scholarships with similar essay prompts, you can submit the same essay with minimal changes. You might need to tweak a few things to fit the new application or add/remove some information, but you'll already have a solid base to work from. This can save you a lot of time and stress. Writing essays can be a lengthy process, so if you can reuse them, when possible, it's definitely worth doing.

Refer to Appendices A and B as examples. I submitted these essays for the Gilman scholarship and for admission to graduate school. Both were successful, but they aren't perfect. We're not aiming for perfection. The reality is, there will always be something you could add, fix, or tweak—but if you keep waiting for it to be perfect, you'll never finish. So do your best, be honest, and trust your work!

QUICK TIPS FOR NOW YOU WRITE

- ❖ Do not rush.

- ❖ Recycle essays for scholarships that have the same prompts/questions.

- ❖ Have at least 3 qualified people proofread your essay and provide feedback.

- ❖ Tell a story with your essay; let the readers know why you deserve the scholarship.

- ❖ The key to producing winning essays are great writing skills, answering the questions and providing what is asked for, taking your time, and proofreading.

Chapter 6

YOU HAVE TO WANT IT

Scholarship searching is a time-consuming task because you want to find and receive all the funding you possibly can for college. When it gets difficult or stressful, what is going to keep you motivated? I understand it can get hard, discouraging, or overwhelming, but think about your end goal. Do you want to get your degree debt-free? Pay off loans? Or limit the number of loans you need to take? What is it that you are striving for? Keep that thought in mind when you are applying for these scholarships, and you feel like quitting. You are not done if you have not reached or surpassed your goal. I understand; I wanted to quit plenty of times when writing scholarship essays and filling out applications. I was overwhelmed, stressed, and exhausted. All I wanted to do was graduate and be done with everything, but the reality was that I didn't want to take out multiple loans and have thousands of dollars worth of debt. I had to think about my personal goals and why I was doing this to keep me motivated. Please understand that the fatigue that you may feel is very valid and that you are not the only one experiencing it. I don't want you to think that you are not worthy or unequipped when the journey gets hard because I have been there, and it gets better. I promise that it is worth the journey of late-night essay writing and multiple essay revisions.

There's no secret trick to getting a scholarship. What I've learned and experienced during my own search is shared here. The most important thing to remember is that no one can want a scholarship more than you do. You're the one who has to put in the effort - no one else will write your essays, search for scholarships, or do the work for you. Winning scholarship money takes hard work, and committees can tell if you've given your best in your essays. So, put everything you've got into your search and essay writing. If a two-page paper stands between you and $5,000, make it the best one you've ever written.

I want you to win! It will be hard, but you can do this, and when you receive multiple scholarships, pat yourself on the back. You did it! The journey may seem never-ending, but the money adds up, and the loan options go down. Do not procrastinate; set big goals and write those essays.

I hope this information has been a blessing and meaningful for you. Many students do not receive the education necessary to find and apply for scholarships. Many of us are taught from a young age that scholarships will find us if we get good grades. While this may be true for some, this was not a reality for me. So, I wrote this book for the student who wants to break the financial curses in their family, go to college debt-free, and not have to take out a substantial loan amount or prove someone wrong. I see you. You can do it because I did, and there is nothing special about me. I just did the work.

May God bless your scholarship search and your college journey.

Acknowledgments

To my husband, thank you for your unwavering love and encouragement. To my mom and dad, your support has shaped me in more ways than I can count. To my grandparents, your wisdom and prayers have been my foundation. To my stepdad, thank you for your kindness and support.

I am beyond grateful for each of you!

2 Timothy 1:7

RESOURCES & TIPS

HOW TO SPOT A SCHOLARSHIP SCAM

1. **Asking for Personal Identifiable Information (PII)**

   ❖ Most scholarship applications do ask for some PII whether it's your name, address, the school you attend, parents' name, etc. However, if the application asks for Banking information or your Social Security Number, it is a scam. You should never have to provide your Social Security (SS) number for a scholarship application, and please never give your Social Security number out unless it is to legitimate sources, in which providing your SS number is applicable. Additionally, providing banking information just to apply for a scholarship is unusual. You may provide this information after being notified about winning the scholarship but never prior.

2. **Unsolicited**

   ❖ If you find that you are being solicited by a site claiming to have a scholarship for you that you may have never heard of or didn't apply for. Not to be confused with awards/scholarships you may receive from an organization in your community or from a school because of your high achievement, etc.

   ❖ These solicitations will likely be from illegitimate sources and sites, which should be avoided.

   ❖ Be careful when clicking on unknown links or sites, as they could be phishing or spam.

3. **You are guaranteed to win.**

   ❖ If you are reached out to by a scholarship or scholarship matching service that says if you do this, you are guaranteed to win, that is likely a scam.

- ❖ Those services are often trying to pocket your money. Scholarships are a part of a competitive process. No one can guarantee that you will win.

4. **Asking for money**

    - ❖ Beware of scholarship applications or services that ask you to pay to apply for a scholarship.

    - ❖ Scholarships are always free to apply for; you do not need to pay to apply for a scholarship.

    - ❖ So, if you see a scholarship application that requires money before applying, do not give them money and do not apply. They will pocket your money, and you will never hear from them again.

SITES TO FIND SCHOLARSHIPS

- Bold.org
- College Board
- Going Merry
- Sallie Mae (Yes, Sallie Mae provides scholarships, too, not just loans!
- Scholarships America
- Scholarships.com
- Scholly
- United Negro College Fund
- Your Prospective University Financial Aid website (Ex: If you want to attend Michigan State University, go to their financial aid website to see what scholarships/grants they offer)

- Your State Government Financial aid site (Ex: If you live in the state of Michigan, search for Michigan Scholarships, and the state Gov site should pop up)

BIBLIOGRAPHY

Bisio, Kyle. "Dual Enrollment vs Concurrent Enrollment: What's the Difference?" MSU Denver, 11 Nov. 2022, https://www.msudenver.edu/dual-enrollment-vs-concurrent-enrollment-whats-the-difference/.

"College Scholarships." Affordable Colleges, 27 July 2021, https://www.affordablecollegesonline.org/financial-aid/scholarships/scholarship-guide/.

Federal Student Aid. https://studentaid.gov/h/apply-for-aid/fafsa. Accessed 21 May 2024.

Student. "What Is GPA? Understanding Its Calculation, Importance and Scales," November 12, 2024. https://www.timeshighereducation.com/student/advice/what-gpa.

"MAC Scholars Program | Multicultural Academic Student Services."Www.Cmich.Edu, https://www.cmich.edu/offices-departments/multicultural-academic-student-services/mac-scholars-program. Accessed 21 May 2024.

"What is Ap? – AP Students." College Board, https://apstudents.collegeboard.org/what-is-ap. Accessed 20 May 2024.

Appendix A

My winning Statement of Purpose for the Gilman Scholarship application in 2019.

  I am D'Shyla Hodge, a senior undergraduate student at Central Michigan University (CMU), and I will be graduating with my bachelor's in science of Psychology in May 2020 and the Cultural and Global studies certificate in African and African Diaspora. I am a Multicultural Advancement (MAC) scholar at CMU and yearly there's an opportunity for MAC scholars to study abroad during the summer, this summer our destination is South Africa. I want to receive the Cultural and Global studies certificate in African and African diaspora because I am very passionate about African and African American history. I love learning more about my history, social inequality, and the trials my ancestors went through for the rights I have today. I try to take as many African history courses as I can, but to receive the cultural and global studies certificate it is also extremely encouraged to go on a study abroad trip that corresponds with your certificate. Knowing this I never truly thought I would be able to get the certificate not only because of cost but also because of how soon I will be graduating. I was worried about taking a study abroad trip because of all the time and dedication it would take from me applying for graduate schools, applying for internships, getting a summer job and if it would set me back academically. In my mind, I have more urgent priorities so going abroad couldn't be an option. I've never been so far away without my family and I must prepare for my next step in life.

      So, when I heard of the study abroad trip to South Africa, I didn't even jump at the opportunity initially because I didn't think I could go. Here was an opportunity for me to go to a place I've always dreamed of, to learn about things that I love and that interest. I was going to pass this opportunity up, but my mom is the person who changed my mind and convinced me to apply for this trip to South Africa. My mom told me that she would not allow me to cheat myself out of an experience of a lifetime. She told me not to worry about my future so much and not to rush through my life and regret not taking advantage of every opportunity that came my way. She said live life in moments and seize every one; I am so glad my mom gave me the extra push to apply for this trip. Had it not been for her encouragement, I would've never taken this leap. Going to South Africa is a chance for me to not only achieve my goal of going to Africa but also expand my learning experience beyond books and lectures.

      The name of this trip is South Africa: In the Footsteps of Nelson Mandela: South Africa Literature, Social Justice, History & Culture. On this trip, I will learn about Nelson Mandela, Gandhi and Biko by taking the 3-credit course English 300/CGL 300. Along with taking this course, I'll be touring places such as the prison Nelson Mandela was in, Nelson Mandela's museum, the Zulu nations, Gandhi's home and more. This is a faculty-led study abroad trip and we will be in South Africa for a span of approximately 4 ½ weeks. During this time I will be going to many provinces and cities such as Gauteng: Pretoria, Johannesburg & Liliesleaf, Soweto, and Lesedi; KwaZulu-Natal: Durban, Hluluwe-Umflozi, Howick, and Pietermaritzburg, Zulu Battlefields; Eastern Cape: Addo, Butterworth, Coffee Bay, East London, Hogsback, Mthatha, King Williams Town, and Port Elizabeth, and Qunu; Western Cape: The Townships— Athlone, Guguletu, Khayelitsha, and Langa, Cape Town, Muizenberg Bay, Stellenbosch, and Robben Island. We have many accommodations such as homestays, hotels/hostels, and apartments. I feel the homestays will make the experience very rich because we're not just staying in hotels, we're purposefully immersing ourselves in a different environment and culture.

    I am thrilled for this learning experience because it grants me the ability to learn by being surrounded by a different environment, and I will gain memories that will last a lifetime. Going to South Africa and taking the ENG 300/CGL 300 course will not only help me get one step further to receiving the

African and African diaspora studies certificate, but I hope it will grant me social skills and an overall new outlook on life that will help me in my productivity and creativity in my classes. I hope this experience will also help with my future career in Public Health by expanding my cultural outlook. This is because being introduced to a new culture and atmosphere, where I will have to learn about how people function and live, is essential to Public Health research. Public health is about community upliftment and advocacy as it pertains to healthcare.

      In this field, it is highly encouraged to travel and immerse yourself in different environments so that you can gain knowledge and research in many ways to find your preferred study in public health. I want to focus on impoverished African American communities by improving their health care systems and advancing their communities. Going to South Africa is a perfect opportunity to observe the environments that South Africans live in and learn more about African and African American history so that I can build on that knowledge to help with the African American communities I will potentially work with. In public health being adaptable, friendly, and knowledgeable about where other people come from is very important when working with new people especially when they are relying on you to help them. This is another reason why I am looking forward to this trip because I believe that it will help me be the best Public Healthcare worker possible.

  Overall, this trip to South Africa is a great opportunity for me to experience a new culture, learn about legendary landmarks and people, and gain knowledge that can only obtain by being there. I am thrilled for this trip because my family is very supportive, they encourage me to seize every opportunity and never give up on my dreams. I desperately want to go to South Africa because it is a once in a lifetime opportunity. I know my family will do what they can to help raise the money for me to attend this study abroad trip. Unfortunately, they do not have the finances to fund this trip, which is approximately 6,000 dollars. Applying for this scholarship is my way of trying to relieve them as much as I can because this trip is very expensive. So, if I was granted this scholarship, it would help my family tremendously so they wouldn't have to strain their finances and penny pinch for me to have this opportunity. If chosen I can assure you that I will fulfill my commitment to your organization and be very appreciative of the reward. Thank you all so much for granting people like myself such a grand opportunity!

Appendix B

My personal statement for admission to my Master of Public Health program.

      I would be an excellent candidate for the Grand Valley State University Master of Public Health program because I have always had a passion for community outreach and empowering my community by expanding their knowledge on health disparities, while also volunteering and doing what I can to better connect with my community. In pursuing my Bachelor of Psychology degree, I realized that becoming a medical doctor was no longer my desire. Although, I loved learning about the human body, improving my critical thinking skills, and being able to help others through health care, the lack of variety bothered me. I needed a career that allowed me to help a variety of people, express my passion for community upliftment through healthcare and social justice, provided a space for open communication and group thinking, while continually pushing me to improve. I knew what I wanted to do but never knew a name for it and after much research I began to learn about a career in public health.

      Furthermore, I took Psychological Statistics and Behavioral Neuroscience courses which improved my critical thinking skills and research ability. Whereas, classes such as Social Inequality and

Racism/Discrimination through dialogue awakened my passion for social justice in impoverished communities, while also nurturing my group skills and ability to carry out a productive discussion. Additionally, I took a study abroad trip to South Africa for 4-weeks and saw first-hand the result of poor nutrition and lack of proper healthcare. In South Africa, I volunteered at many schools where most of the children only ate during school due to the high rate of unemployment in their communities. This motivated me to expand my knowledge on public health and what I can do in my very own community. These experiences confirm my growing interest in community outreach, quality healthcare, and improving communities by incorporating better knowledge about nutrition. Therefore, I know I will be a strong candidate for this program because of my undergraduate experience and growing determination.

    The GVSU MPH program is the best program for me because it promotes impactful learning about public health in all communities while also incorporating teamwork and community outreach so that students can apply what they are learning to real-life situations. This program embodies everything I could ask for in an MPH program. The option to study health promotion is perfect because this emphasis will increase my knowledge on health disparities in diverse communities, teach me how to promote healthcare and navigate public health by social campaigning and applying it to different communities to improve their way of life. I know that being a part of this program will help me achieve my goals of furthering my education in public health because this program strives for each student to gain knowledge in the classroom while also incorporating hands-on learning through community collaboration and research with faculty. If accepted into this program, I will bring cooperative group membership, great listening skills, determination, passion, great communication skills and great writing skills.

With my emphasis area of interest being health promotion, my expectation for my career in public health is to apply for positions in the World Health Organization, Center for Disease Control and Prevention, shelters in my community and more. Studying Health promotion will increase my knowledge on health disparities in diverse communities while teaching me how to promote health, navigate public health by social campaigning, and how to apply it to different communities to improve their way of life. With this knowledge, I want to work in an environment where I can learn what the people in the community truly lack as it relates to health care and social justice, while also learning how an effective community center operates. So, I can ultimately build a community center in my hometown Flint, MI that will serve as a place to educate the people in my community on proper physical, mental, and emotional health.

www.ingramcontent.com/pod-product-compliance
Lightning Source LLC
Chambersburg PA
CBHW050520100526